A Bald Eagle's World

written and illustrated by Caroline Arnold

PICTURE WINDOW BOOKS
a capstone imprint

Special thanks to our advisers for their expertise:

Dr. Dan A. Hart, Executive Trustee
American Bald Eagle Foundation

Terry Flaherty, Ph.D., Professor of English
Minnesota State University, Mankato

Editor: Jill Kalz
Designers: Abbey Fitzgerald and Lori Bye
Art Director: Nathan Gassman
Production Specialist: Jane Klenk
The illustrations in this book were created with cut paper.

Picture Window Books
151 Good Counsel Drive
P.O. Box 669
Mankato, MN 56002-0669
877-845-8392
www.picturewindowbooks.com

Printed in the United States of America in North Mankato, Minnesota.
092009
005618CGS10

 All books published by Picture Window Books
are manufactured with paper containing at least
10 percent post-consumer waste.

Library of Congress Cataloging-in-Publication Data
Arnold, Caroline.
A bald eagle's world / written and illustrated by Caroline Arnold.
p. cm. — (Caroline Arnold's animals)
Includes index.
ISBN 978-1-4048-5741-4 (library binding)
1. Bald eagle—Juvenile literature. I. Title.
QL696.F32A757 2010
598.9'42—dc22   2009033358

Bald Eagles

Where they live: United States, Canada, northern Mexico

Habitat: near lakes, rivers, marshes, and seacoasts

Food: fish, birds, small mammals, carcasses of dead animals

Body length: 28 to 38 inches (71 to 97 centimeters)

Weight: 6.6 to 15 pounds (3 to 6.8 kilograms)

Wingspan: 6 to 8 feet (1.8 to 2.4 meters)

Animal class: birds

Scientific name: *Haliaeetus leucocephalus*

All baby birds are called chicks. Baby eagles are also called eaglets. Follow two eaglets through their first year of life and learn about a bald eagle's world.

It is spring in Alaska. In a tall tree, bald eagles are building a nest. Soaring on wide wings, the male eagle brings a big stick. The female eagle weaves it into the nest.

4

They add more sticks and
make a huge platform. They
put in moss and feathers to
make the nest soft. Now it is
ready for eggs.

Bald eagle nests are about the size of a large
bed. They are 6 to 7 feet (1.8 to 2.1 m) across.
Bald eagles build the biggest nests of any bird.

The female eagle lays one egg in the nest. The next day she lays another. The male and female eagles take turns sitting on the eggs. They keep the eggs warm and safe.

An eagle egg is about the size of a tennis ball. It is 2.9 inches (7.4 cm) long and 2.2 inches (5.6 cm) wide.

Inside each egg, an eagle chick is growing. In five weeks, the eggs will hatch.

Peep! Peep! The first eagle chick is ready to come out of its egg. It pushes hard against the thick shell. It makes a tiny hole. It pushes again and again. Finally, the shell cracks open.

The next day, the second egg hatches. *Peep! Peep!* call the tiny birds. They are hungry. Their parents feed them small pieces of fish.

An eagle chick breaks its shell with an egg tooth. The egg tooth is a pointed knob on the top of a chick's beak. After the chick hatches, its egg tooth falls off.

9

The mother and father eagles take turns finding food for their growing chicks. One parent stays in the nest while the other hunts.

moose

From high above the river, the eagle spots food. It swoops down and grabs a fish with its feet. Strong claws, or talons, help grip the slippery fish. The eagle brings it back to the nest and shares it with the chicks.

An eagle has super eyesight. It can see an animal the size of a rabbit from up to 1 mile (1.6 km) away.

11

grizzly
bear

The eagle chicks grow quickly. By 1 month old, they can walk around the nest. Long feathers are starting to grow on their legs and tails. During the day, the young birds stay alone while both parents hunt for food.

Adult bald eagles have no natural predators. Sometimes eagle eggs or chicks are taken by other birds, bears, or raccoons.

At night, their mother joins them in the nest. She keeps them warm and safe. The father rests on a branch nearby.

The eagle chicks are now almost 3 months old. They are as big as their parents. Smooth, dark feathers cover their bodies. They flap their wings and jump on the edge of the nest.

One chick spreads its wings. A gust of wind lifts it into the air. Suddenly the chick is flying. It lands on a branch nearby. Soon the other chick will leave the nest, too.

Young eagles are fed by their parents for about two months after they leave the nest.

The young eagles become strong fliers. They follow their parents. They watch them hunt for fish, rabbits, and other birds.

16

Swooping and pouncing, the young eagles practice hunting. By the age of 5 months, they can catch their own food. They are ready to live on their own.

Eagles are fast fliers. They can fly up to 30 miles (48 km) per hour and dive at 100 miles (160 km) per hour.

The days are getting shorter. The first snow has fallen, and the river is starting to freeze. It is time for the young eagles to fly to the coast. They find many other eagles there. All winter long, the birds hunt for fish in the ocean.

When spring comes, the adult eagles fly back to their nests. The young birds find their own territories.

In winter, eagles often come together where food is plentiful. During the rest of the year, they stay in their own territories.

The young eagles are now almost a year old. They have new brown feathers. Each year they will grow a new set of feathers.

In four years, the young eagles' heads and tails will be white. The birds will look just like their parents. They will be ready to find mates, build nests, and raise their own chicks. Then more bald eagles will soar high in the sky.

Where do bald eagles live?

Bald eagles live in Canada, northern Mexico, and every state of the United States except Hawaii. More eagles live in Alaska than anywhere else. Some eagles stay in the same place year round. Others migrate in winter to areas where food is more plentiful. For many years, the bald eagle was on the U.S. government list of Endangered and Threatened Wildlife. It was taken off the list on June 28, 2007.

Alaska

Canada

United States

Mexico

where bald eagles live

Bald Eagle Fun Facts

Symbol of the United States
The bald eagle is the national bird of the United States. It is on the national seal. It holds an olive branch in one foot and arrows in the other foot. A seal is a mark used on official government papers.

Not Bald
Many people believe bald eagles got their name from the Old English word balde, meaning "white." The scientific name for the bald eagle, Haliaeetus leucocephalus, means "white-headed sea bird."

Mates for Life
A bald eagle pair stays together for their whole lives. If one of them dies, the other eagle finds a new mate.

Long Lives
Eagles in the wild may live to be 30 years old. In zoos, they may live as long as 50 years.

Who Is Bigger?
The bald eagle is the largest bird of prey in North America. As in most predatory birds, the female is about one-third larger than the male.

Sharp Talons
An eagle has four toes, three facing forward and one backward. Its claws, or talons, are 2 to 4 inches (5 to 10 cm) long. They are needle sharp.

Giant Nest
The biggest eagle nest ever found was in Florida. It was 20 feet (6.1 m) deep, 9.5 feet (2.9 m) wide, and weighed almost 3 tons (2.7 metric tons).

The Most Birds
Alaska has about 55,000 bald eagles—more than the entire lower 48 states combined.

Glossary

bird of prey—*a bird that hunts other animals for its food*

carcass—*the dead body of an animal*

egg tooth—*the horny knob on the top of a beak used by a bird to break out of its shell*

habitat—*the place and natural conditions in which a plant or animal lives*

mammal—*a warm-blooded animal that feeds its young milk*

mate—*a male or female of a pair of animals*

migrate—*to regularly move from one place to another to find food, shelter, or a mate; some animals migrate with the seasons.*

predator—*an animal that hunts and eats other animals*

prey—*an animal that is hunted and eaten by another animal*

talon—*the claw of a bird of prey*

territory—*the area in which an animal lives*

To Learn More

More Books to Read

Landau, Elaine. *The Bald Eagle*. New York: Children's Press, 2008.

Pearl, Norman. *The Bald Eagle*. Minneapolis: Picture Window Books, 2007.

Stone, Lynn M. *Bald Eagle*. Vero Beach, Fla.: Rourke Pub., 2004.

Internet Sites

FactHound offers a safe, fun way to find Internet sites related to this book. All of the sites on FactHound have been researched by our staff.

Here's all you do:

Visit *www.facthound.com*

FactHound will fetch the best sites for you!

Index

photo by Arthur Arnold

Caroline Arnold is the author of more than 100 books for children. Her books have received awards from the American Library Association, P.E.N., the National Science Teachers Association, and the Washington Post/Children's Book Guild.

Caroline's interest in animals and the outdoors began when she was a child growing up in Minnesota. After majoring in art and literature at Grinnell College in Iowa, she received her M.A. in art from the University of Iowa.

Caroline lives in Los Angeles with her husband, Art, a neuroscientist. They enjoy traveling and bird-watching and have observed bald eagles in Alaska and the lower 48 states.

Look for all of the books in Caroline Arnold's Animals series:

A Bald Eagle's World   *A Penguin's World*

A Kangaroo's World   *A Platypus' World*

A Killer Whale's World   *A Polar Bear's World*

A Koala's World   *A Walrus' World*

A Moose's World   *A Wombat's World*

A Panda's World   *A Zebra's World*